SONGS OF IMMORTALITY

Other books by Solee MacIsaac

Joy Shared
A Beloved Speck in the Universe
Little Wisdoms
Zen Days, Zen Nights
Harvest

Songs of Immortality

Solee MacIsaac

EVERY BOOK PRESS
MMXXIV

© Copyright 2024 Solee MacIsaac
All rights reserved.
ISBN: 978-0-9837714-9-4

Book Design:
William Bentley

INTRODUCTION

Although it is not possible for words to convey the lofty aim of this title, nonetheless these short poems humbly attempt the impossible. As a note: The "You" referred to in these poems is meant to be a direction to myself.

Solee MacIsaac

These words are dedicated to the Fellowship of Friends, without which I could not thrive.

Thank you: To my husband for his tireless editing, and endless support. He is an excellent writer, champion husband, and besides all of that, he is a Laird. He owns one cubic foot of land in Scotland.

*Fill your heart
With a bouquet of
Rose-petaled love notes.*

SONGS OF IMMORTALITY

Wind whips,
Wings shred,
Buoyancy drops.

Fall on your knees,
Hear the angels' voices;
Oh, night divine.

The climb to Heaven
May be arduous,
But oh, so worth it.

We salute you,
You who fought and won
The mighty battle.

Bright rays shine forth
From the nimbus
Of the belovéd.

Bask in the afterglow
Of the eternal fire
Combusting in Cupid's heart.

Love is eternal,
Though not always visited
Upon a hard heart.

Life continues
And is immortal,
But not always embodied.

Wings spread,
Ready to fly;
Drop unnecessary weight.

Distant voices
Vague, mysterious,
Beckoning us home.

Infinite wisdom
Stems from
Eternal patience.

Want nothing
And you shall have it –
Nothing.

Worldly unity,
Unrealistic.
Inner unity, possible.

Nature does not express
Negative emotions,
Humans imitate each other.

Rising above
Cacophony of voices
Is the simplicity of silence.

Sweetest refrain
Drifting on starlight,
Guiding me home.

Living forever
Without the gift of forgetting,
Torture beyond reckoning.

Lifting above earthly issues
Cold stratosphere
Of non-possession endures.

Eternal being
Is for Gods,
Not for temporal mortals.

Beyond the veil
Lies infinite reality:
Lift it.

Grasp light tendrils,
Weave together
Your astral body.

Birth, growth, reproduction, death,
Life cycle;
Squared by self-awareness.

Cross of burden
Is pierced by ascending
Column of light.

Light shines down on
Garden of light;
Rainbow colors return the favor.

Arguments,
Like a cosmic storm,
Blow over, eventually.

The body's mind –
You can fight with what it wants,
But not with what it needs.

Failure is one
Of the repeated
Steps to success.

Gripping the present moment,
Is like grasping water,
It follows its own laws.

The challenge can be
Overwhelming,
Progress is moment by moment.

Mind, soul, spirit,
Human body of Earth,
But mostly starlight.

Sailing on cosmic fumes,
Watching galaxies form,
Timeless and body-less.

Enlightened One,
We follow your trail of light
From now to now.

Galaxies are formed,
Dissolved,
And reformed through millennia.

Who sees it all?
Who is there for it to matter,
That the show goes on?

Intermix of molecules
From mollusk to mountain,
Intricate designs decorate Earth.

A privilege to receive
The exalted view,
Of angels' handiwork.

O Earth, mother of all existing,
O Sun, father of life and breath,
O Moon, child of stability and change.

Listen. In the silence,
Your heart beats,
To the cosmic rhythm.

To live beyond the body
Requires building
A new one.

Create a body of mist
And whispers,
But mostly light.

Grace is bestowed
On the humble,
Wealth on the less fortunate.

Making efforts,
Like losing weight,
Is a hard won success.

Listening is different,
When inner space
Is silent.

Long thoughts and plans
May be useful,
But not by displacing presence.

Our true parents
Love us without reservation;
Re-education is a relentless must.

The Ideal State
Circulates within
The golden initiated.

Unfold your wings,
Breathe deeply,
Let your song soar forth to Heaven.

Dawn greets the early riser,
Morning warms
Bird singers with ancient light.

Other worlds
May have different customs,
But the same laws.

Each rung of the ladder
Holds a new experience,
To transform.

Be quick, be still,
This moment flees;
Stay with it, gladly.

We have not lost,
Who have gained presence
In this moment.

A transparent silhouette
Of sweetest light
Embodies my perfect love.

Rest your deepest longing,
In the cushion of certainty,
All is as it should be.

Endless love pours forth from above,
More than our mere hearts can hold.
Share the abundant wealth.

Harp and piano,
Gorgeous melody
Bursts fountains of light.

I opened my eyes
To a falling star over the ocean,
Wondering who waked me.

Make your guiding light
Be the ever-present dome,
Of the bright awakened.

Lemon, ice, pure water, honey,
Recipe for "ade,"
That aids in hot weather.

A common flower
Is not so common,
Just look at it.

Summer breezes hold
Floral fragrances,
Tempting lone hearts to meld.

Love is a long hard road
With many potholes,
But worth the journey.

Nuptials are held
For the bride and groom,
Psyche and Cupid unite in joy.

Wake the belovéd,
It is time to evolve,
Chrysalis broken open.

The veil is thinnest,
When closest to
This present moment.

We cannot understand
Eternity, infinity, immortality,
Our faculties are not capable.

We can experience
Many things
Without words.

Strands of music,
Pure and resounding,
Heighten existence.

Art in its many forms
Reminds us of our true place,
And real home.

It is sad that we must be reminded
To be grateful,
The very air we breathe is gifted.

Morning: a new opportunity
To kiss the hem of Demeter's
Flowery gown.

Tracing the path
That leads to hidden respite,
Where inside treasures are shielded.

All that we are,
Cannot imagine
What we may become.

There are no secrets,
Only misplaced moments
Of untrusted truths.

Radiant love
Lifts us above
So-called normalcy.

When Love takes hold,
We seem crazy,
Responding to different laws.

To love all,
Is to operate in the medium
Of Gods.

Outside of time,
Things are not static,
But charged with eternal existence.

We love whom we can,
Are kind to many,
And accept the rest.

How different
To have love flow endlessly
To everyone.

Our two hands work together
Simpatico,
So should our heart and mind.

When the master is home,
The house runs
Beautifully.

Roses fill our life with joy,
Love fills our soul
With presence.

Capture beauty
In your heart,
Whenever, wherever you find it.

To love presence
Enables many opportunities
To externally consider others.

We are loved unconditionally,
Our spirits are composed
Of loving light.

Sing, lift your eyes to the sky,
Let the best sound reverberate,
Call on Heaven to open her gates.

We are mere reflections
From the invisible sphere
Of what is real.

Difficult to conceive
Superior beings;
They have no problem conceiving us.

Don't fret, if feeling lonely,
It is only an illusion,
Like so many others.

We are not sheltered from pain,
But given every chance to transform
And keep on the fated path.

Love is not always shown as
Soft kisses,
But through consistent care.

Time affords more opportunities
To be consistent,
Sustained by heart action.

Infinite reality,
Eternal beauty,
Medium of immortals.

Harmony of choral singers,
Union of voices lifted,
Praising highest Light.

We love to the extent
That we can
Be present.

Negativity
Is a lower level of consciousness
Than when asleep in bed.

The eternal light
Of awakened hearts
Has space for all who bask.

Uncreated light
Fosters hierarchy
Of correct levels of inner mastery.

Be strong, be flexible,
Be ready, be present,
Be nothing at all.

The no face,
And no mind,
Are everything.

Angels don't need
Mouths,
To sing love and praise.

Heartfelt devotion
Is light-years ahead
Of facts.

Is it living to walk, breathe, talk?
In one moment,
We can live forever.

Death is the greatest
Illusion,
More troublesome than birth.

We cheer over a newborn,
And cry at a gravesite,
From whence did we come and go?

The invisible realm
Teaches the visible realm,
In a thousand subtle ways.

Voice and heart
Are connected,
Revealed by singing.

Listen carefully,
Voices tell much more
Than they are saying.

Immortality
Is not connected
With this Earth level.

Walt Whitman
Sang the body electric,
He is probably still singing it.

Diamond facets
Reflect light in many directions,
A radiant creation.

Hours, days, moments,
Are short or infinitely long,
Depending on our state.

Rest is better achieved
With an uncluttered
Mind.

I trust a winged message,
Ultimate gift;
Open it.

Rituals enacted,
Can go deep,
Reflecting a higher order.

Prayer, if heartfelt,
Can reveal one's
Unreserved hopes and fears.

There really is only one
Shakespeare,
How could there be another.

Another morning,
Why does it create fear?
The march to death is inevitable.

The glory of existence
Is palpable,
If you are there to receive it.

It's a heavy load to lift,
All your baggage;
Must be dropped to ascend.

Baby birds must be taught
To fly,
Baby angels, also.

Respect your Self,
So much has been invested
In You.

Iridescent wings flutter before me,
Reminder of
Angelic assistance.

Helping others
To the path,
Helps oneself as well.

Without outside help,
All is
For naught.

They lift us smoothly,
Even if we don't
Relish the view.

Angel light
Pervades the heavens,
Illuminating gossamer beings.

Touring our galaxy
In an eye blink,
Angels work with fewer laws.

To join the ranks of elevated beings,
Make humility and service
Your virtues.

Small efforts in the moment
Outweigh
The grand gesture.

Love's breeze
Can stir a cyclone
In a willing heart.

The road to heaven
Is paved
With sparkling conscious moments.

Fears hold us back,
Courage and fortitude,
Help sustain consistent efforts.

Remember we have help;
Even if we don't always recognize it,
Love never falters.

Many mirrors
Accompany our journey,
Seeing oneself, a necessity.

A lantern in the dark
Shines only a small distance;
Unite with everlasting light.

It is important to trust,
And,
To tie your camel.

Clean, harmonious,
Present in the moment,
Pure of imagination.

The love light
In your eyes
Alights mine instantly.

An aromatic garden is the closest
To the abode of angels,
Harmony of color and fragrance.

Sweep the ground with your hair,
The pathway must be clear
For the steps of the belovéd.

Ecstatic singing
Surrounds the Aurora
Of the highest angel.

No amount of gratitude
Can ever be enough,
For the greatest gift of all.

The radiant one
Guides our inner life,
The outer one less important.

Between the brows
The diamond sits,
Third eye receiving all.

We are lost
Without the compass,
Given with otherworldly grace.

Melodic strands of purest sound
Carry the message,
To receptive ears.

Lower your barriers,
Not your standards,
Elevate your aspirations.

Finest energies can
Create babies,
Or eternal spirit bodies.

Love fully, deeply,
Don't hold back,
What can you lose, really?

Lift your voice,
Join hearts in song,
Praising the belovéd.

Spirit wind
Blows kindly,
Over an ocean of love.

The finish on a fine wine,
Can bring smiles
To ruby lips.

Fill your cup
And then keep pouring,
Overflowing abundance is yours.

The breath of Earth,
Ebbs and flows,
Carrying tidings of cosmic changes.

Everything makes a sound,
Even the smallest body
Makes tiny notes on Nature's lute.

Booming harmony of planets
Sends sound waves through
Our solar system.

Loud or soft,
The amazing concert
Eternally continues.

Love notes
Sound the very best,
Open your ears to bliss.

Wings of light
Lift full heart and empty mind
To the stars.

Grazing in green pastures
Simple sheep
Grow white wooly coats.

Nature, if unperturbed,
Is perfection
Of balance and beauty.

Even the eternal
Optimist
Meets Death eventually.

Music soothes the beast,
Opens the heart,
And teaches harmonious order.

In the hierarchy of angels,
Archangels
Create archetypes.

Don't hold back,
Live on the very edge of yourself,
Time slips all into oblivion.

Essence can feel hurt,
But no real damage is done;
Relinquish imagination.

Grace in adversity,
Is sometimes just
Holding one's tongue.

Send as much love
As you can,
To all you know.

Rodney Collin
Knew the strength
Of positive emotions.

Leaping over your own knees
Is not impossible,
Just leave your body behind.

Sometimes we smile
At people we don't like;
Drop insincerity, try compassion.

One's own death reveals
The illusions
Of life.

Non-attachment
Does not mean giving things away,
But to not give your Self away.

To be angelic
Is not to be sweetness,
But to be a warrior of inner truth.

Cradle what is most precious,
Weld it to your brow;
Keep looking, listening. Stay silent.

The more we try,
The more we are helped,
So fortunate to win by failing.

Look for your Self
In the mirror,
Around every corner.

Stop! Who is looking?
Why are you searching?
Rest in deep realization of love.

A knife is for cutting,
Sever the connection
To this sleepy world.

Our senses are meager tools
To grasp the Almighty heavenly host;
Best to empty mind and fill heart.

No one is too humble,
Or great, or old, or young,
For inner work.

Uncreated light covers everyone
Who can experience it,
Who can cherish it.

Eternity is a wholeness,
The moment is a movement within;
Stay with the moment, bypass time.

Eternal life,
If it exists,
Must involve service.

Learning may be difficult,
But not as challenging
As un-learning.

The world values experiences,
Make yours profitable
Toward your aim.

Many things are not in our control.
Focus on what you can control,
Leave the rest to angels.

Moment to moment,
We pick our way,
To divine Presence.

Fellow students on the path
Can be of great assistance,
Or amazing denying force.

Each of us
Has a play
That must be followed.

The light of the Earth
Is strong and vital,
The light of Heaven is divine.

Supposedly, it is dark inside bodies,
But since our nerves are electric,
We must light up like Christmas trees.

Few things are as they seem,
Staying as simple as possible
Reduces blunders.

Touching a higher world
Can have lasting effects,
Making sleep much less attractive.

Be who you truly are,
Not who you think you should be;
Each moment is a new challenge.

Bathe in the glory
Of the shining present,
Effort and reward are immediate.

We can do nothing real,
Without the necessary assistance
Of our divine guides.

No amount of gratitude
Can balance the generous help
Of benevolent angelic beings.

Keep the flame of
Inside and outside awareness
Alive within your sacred space.

The illusion of time is strong,
It takes a special effort
To slip between breaths.

Death is final,
For this collection of experiences,
But not for the experiencer.

The little old person
Hiding inside the infant
Is revealed in the depth of baby eyes.

Cosmic dust
Filters down to us,
Every day, each moment.

We are part of this universe,
Not separate,
Not alone.

The conscious spark
Flickers from eye to eye,
Keep yours burning.

Courage in the face
Of imaginary obstacles,
Is still courage.

This moment is not dull;
Asleep to its offerings,
Again missing opportunities.

Efforts and reminders are repeated,
As our state is like an elevator,
All depends on which floor you land.

Dip your wings in the love font,
Shake them out,
Spray sweet drops to fevered brows.

We crave love,
But squirm under its dictates:
Embrace all under Love's umbrella.

Counting, timing, rhythm,
Music has rules,
Sustaining its soaring emotions.

Payment is required
For everything of value,
Prioritize your choices.

Each part of you has different
Preferences,
Become whole to be clear-headed.

Children learn love
By being loved,
Love as a force is so much stronger.

We are in this together,
Rocking the boat is risky
For all.

The world is heating up,
Tempers may rise,
All influences can be used for work.

Words point to images,
Which can hold emotional sparks,
And may be easily absorbed.

Scent of a Summer storm,
An ancient memory from the East,
Flickers through my memory.

Old friends,
Even untouched in ages,
Remain deeply connected.

Scrubbing, cleaning,
Seems endless and repetitive,
But has a positive result.

A generous gift of fresh flowers,
Delights both the giver
And the receiver.

We are pressed upon
To stay present,
The pressure is needed.

Although sacrifice is necessary,
Mostly what is relinquished
Is imaginary.

The sweetest strands
From a violin,
Cannot compare with angelic music.

Traveling and sightseeing
Expand our perception of this world,
But not the next.

Climbing the ladder,
A worthy effort;
Don't look down.

Saints and sages
Have travelled this way before us,
Many rocks and obstacles removed.

Wise words may fill our prayers;
We know action is necessary,
To create real being.

Being the words,
Sometimes the most
Difficult task to fulfill.

Full realization of one's being
Releases immeasurable
Compassion.

Nature's beautiful gift
Fills the senses,
Sumptuous exquisite roses.

Young hearts
And old souls
Unite in masterful artistry.

In the shrinking light,
Most things pale in death,
Not Autumn's leaf.

Toast to this life,
This body, mind, soul,
Next time is another story.

Bright flashes of angel light
Show in an instant
A world much larger than realized.

A white cygnet on a blue pond,
Charming reminder that
We will grow into elegant swans.

Let go and fly,
Earth can only hold you
For so long.

Waiting can make time slow,
Fun times can speed it up,
The clock in our heads ticks away.

Friends gather
To celebrate
Their joyful sharing.

We have so little time, really,
When you count
By conscious moments.

We exist in the lower levels
Of creation,
But have incredible possibilities.

Love the one you are with,
And all the others as well,
Love is contagious.

Competition is silly
Unless it is with
Your previous level of competence.

We are each designed
For specific endeavors,
Hence: the Play.

Laugh at yourself,
Rather than criticize,
Skip one level of denying force.

Madness abounds,
Within and without,
Make yours divine.

If we focus on what we have lost
By aging,
Imagination will take root.

Sheltered in the undying light,
We group together,
And sing our gratitude.

Wings flutter
And blend before my eyes:
Am I seeing, what I'm seeing?

No amount of decoration
Can pretty-up,
A sleeping fate.

Essence needs nothing
To enhance
Its particular beauty.

Though not immortal,
Essence
Can assist esoteric progress.

Pull up your bootstraps,
We are going swimming,
In a Sea of Love.

We won't sink,
Being lighter than air
We will rise to the stars.

Walt Whitman rested in grass,
And told his tales of
Love, light, and extraordinary being.

We walk on the graves of history,
Millennia of humans,
Born, lived, died, long before us.

Few have left traces
With impact,
Ordinary is the norm.

Let your personal mark be
To have loved everyone fully,
Within your earthly sphere.

The closer my death follows me,
The more generous and loving
I am allowed to be.

Good News!
The All and Everything
Invites you to your real Self.

Throw open the gates,
Immortality awaits,
The pure and simple.

A diamond ring?
A chateau in France?
Make your treasure timeless.

Perfection of mind and body
Raises eyebrows
But not souls to heaven.

Sitting on a throne
Will not improve your chances,
The price is more than your kingdom.

Sinners unite,
Pledge your wayward lives
To higher service.

What is more
Is usually less;
Reverse complicated thinking.

The Ideal to aspire to
May already be near at hand,
Raise your eyes.

A split second
Can change everything,
We cannot afford to sleep.

Prepare for the honored guest,
The more awake in serving,
The more awake in receiving.

We are granted what we can
Maintain and care for,
Much more would be downfall.

Good parents monitor
What the child can handle,
Our real parents serve us just so.

Heavenly light surrounds us
With divine awareness,
Hearts join in gratitude.

Crystals form slowly,
Then all at once,
Like clear conscious reality.

Protect what you most value,
Risk the rest,
Leap off the edge and fly.

The blaze of Heaven
Can blind he who has not
Purified his vessel.

Light pierces space and time,
But heavy dense obstacles
Dim its radiance.

To fill your body with light,
Release all thoughts,
Empty your desires.

Love the questions
With open heart,
Be the answers.

We dance to celebrate
Our lives together,
We sing to reach our highest Selves.

It seems strange
That we should be so lucky;
Only Gods can understand.

The mysterious luck
That everybody wants,
Only for few to have.

Luck or not,
There is work
To be done.

Cherubs decorate
Columns and cornices,
Baby angels watching over us.

Tipping the scales,
One feather
Can change the balance.

The aim of self-seeing
Is good,
But who is looking?

Connect to the song of your life,
It will all go easier,
Don't fight what is rightfully yours.

Sometimes we are ashamed
To recognize our true Selves,
We do not feel worthy.

One does not need to preach
To be one's true Self,
Only to love and be grateful.

Lucky birds fly closer to Heaven,
Feather light,
Air movement aids their flight.

A shower of white blossoms
In a fading orchard
Lands on my hair and face.

Anything can remind
Of the need for
Presence.

Taking inner time and space
For Presence,
Can mean displacing pushy urges.

What seemed funny yesterday,
Seems only mildly absurd today,
Will it be irrelevant tomorrow?

Gather your garments,
Lift your sandals,
Stretch your wings to the heights.

Great things await
The virtues of
Patience and perseverance.

Comparisons with others' plays
Is probably not helpful,
Each of us has a unique opportunity.

God light, Presence, Love,
Self-realization, gratitude,
What else is needed?

The whirlwind of life
Can turn us around,
Come back to the center of being.

Dreams can guide us,
Or just eliminate digested images;
Sleep is not always restful.

If we were aware
Of who truly guides us,
Our lives would dramatically change.

A cushion of rose petals
Could not soothe
The insatiable queens.

The privilege to pay,
And receive the prize,
Is beyond measure incredible.

There is an infinite spark
Allotted to us,
Of god-like perception.

The phrase "use it or lose it"
Comes into play.
Stay home.

Bow low,
Before
The Belovéd.

Pure silence
Is profound
Respect.

Sometimes tears come easily,
Other times we cannot feel anything,
Surface emotions are changeable.

Put your positive emotions to work,
Rein in the erratic horse
And consciously Love.

Alert to others' needs,
Acting swiftly and gracefully,
May also assist one's Self.

Cherubs are sweet;
Angels can carry swords,
Don't underestimate their power.

Accept what lies in your path,
Transform
The expression of negativity.

The beauty you see
Must be inside you
In order to appreciate it.

The whisper of a kiss,
A fragrant breeze,
A love note in my ear.

I can't see you,
But I know you are near,
Love continually beckons.

You don't have to do everything,
Just because you can;
Stop and think, first.

Innocence can be useful,
But not,
Naïveté.

Mind can be
A good tool,
If it does not run amok.

You can't wait to be
In your safe space,
To attempt presence.

Sunlight falls on everyone,
You don't need to be special,
To benefit from Nature's gifts.

Making efforts in areas
Others cannot recognize,
Also not special, but extraordinary.

Open all the doors,
Let in light and air,
Fresh existence awaits.

We feel stale and old,
If our patterns never vary;
Presence is the fountain of youth.

It is not so much morals,
But common sense,
And priority of valuation.

If you feel hot and tired,
Splash cool water of truth,
Over your psyche.

At the end of your
Rope?
Let go.

Help is running to your aid,
Even if you can't
Recognize it.

Laws in our universe
Affect everything material:
Motion, waves and particles.

Our swirling existence
Is subject to entropy,
Extra effort is required to ascend.

To save your life,
Breathe,
To save your soul, Love.

In some ways,
It is a strange combination,
Body, mind, soul, spirit.

We take for granted
That all is in its appropriate order.
A dangerous assumption.

Plato wrote laws,
Rilke needed no more Springs,
We have so much help.

Whining or praising,
Climb as high as you can,
The Gods will do the rest.

We are so lucky
To be allowed to pay
For the privilege of higher states.

The phenomenon of
Two-way seeing
Makes observing exponential.

Truth, not easily captured,
Remains unbidden
By most.

After years of efforts,
Spontaneous reality suddenly
Lights up inner space.

Do not be discouraged,
A stout heart is strong support
For sustained efforts.

Creation can be beautiful,
Maintenance not so much,
Yet necessary on this level.

Maintenance of each one of us
Must be an act of love,
By dedicated angelic workers.

If we learn one thing
In this grand experiment,
Let it be to Love.

"Winging it" implies
You are high enough
To see what is ahead.

The future and the past
Exist only in Eternity,
Our existence is only in this moment.

To know reality,
Lead the life
Of higher centers.

Even in Summer,
A chocolate brownie brings a smile
To hot grumpy people.

The concept of an angel
Assigned specifically to oneself
May be difficult to comprehend.

A conscious play
Is ordained from above,
Payment has been in advance.

Try to relax,
Even while concentrating,
All is connected and affected.

Pressure is inevitable,
Leave it all behind,
Arise to open space.

The paradox of effort
Versus effortless,
Depends upon state.

When You are home,
There is no need for
Longing and striving.

Rejoice, there is peace
Within the halls of silence,
Light pervades this holy place.

There is no 'I'
To solve problems,
All must be swept away by Love.

Friends encourage
Our quiet shared inner space,
Gods provide the light.

We are not really doing
Much of anything,
Except being grateful for our luck.

Jack and Jill went up the hill,
To fetch a pail of truth,
Then tumbled down to self.

Intercepting wayward
Emotions
Requires far-sighted vision.

Just like chores and maintenance,
Last minute fixes
Can be inefficient and unsuccessful.

Birds seem not to suffer
The lack of arms,
Winging into high blue air.

Responsible to keep body well,
Healthy and maintained,
But what is needed for higher Self?

Nothing here,
Can serve there,
All must be transformed.

Here,
Is,
Reality.

Am I greedy for light?
So be it.
More light.

Every change anywhere,
Affects everything else everywhere,
Universe is one, whole.

We are not the children
Of an angry god,
God and anger is an oxymoron.

Habitual negativity
May seem harmless,
How easily we are misled.

Whether swearing at traffic,
Or bemoaning outcast state,
The qualifier is energy lost.

Fortunately, patterns observed
Makes new understandings
A possible result.

Escape the curse
Of your heavy burdens;
Take flight.

School is a shining diamond,
Not in the night sky,
But right here on this Earth.

The love flame,
Resides within hearts
Infused with Presence.

The higher order
Is exactly that,
Superior and organized.

This level is chaotic,
And largely accidental,
Real intelligence is somewhere else.

Truth may seem bitter,
But is merely
Reality without illusions.

How to be grateful
Enough,
For this extraordinary gift?

Awareness of how easily lost
Priceless treasure can be
In a sleeping moment – helps.

Beyond life of the Earth,
Shining entities
Express their joy in song.

Wordless meaning,
Powerful. Fluid.
As Love itself.

Feeling adrift? Uncertain?
Trust who You love most,
And who loves You.

Voice from the heart
Has a different tone,
From any other sound.

Like birds, angels have wings;
Birds have beautiful voices, while
Angels' songs are silently exquisite.

Nature can't really
Compare with the
Supernatural.

The spiral of our lives,
In the conscious cycle,
Is nine times blessed.

Come to my house,
Sit on my cushion,
Rest your mind in sweet harmony.

Vacation is a good word,
Be vacant of all imaginings,
Leave old troubles and fly.

Soft murmurs
Behind the screen,
Mystery. Don't be allured.

Make presence
Your shield,
As well as your love.

Show your true colors
Like the flowers,
Unashamed to be.

Not everything is designed
To be pleasant,
There is a way to stay even.

Meteor showers, Earth's magnetism,
Moon cycles, cosmic influences,
So much is not under our control.

Our little blue haven
Is subject to macro streams
Of fiery sun spouts and flying rocks.

Abrasions at Earth level
Can affect mere mortals,
Even if unperceived.

We don't need tsunamis
To feel pressure,
Our inner worlds are full to brimming.

Compassion and extra care
Are often needed,
Both internally and externally.

We are the fruit
Of the Gods,
Juicy and almost ripe.

Last is not bad,
To be included
Is more than enough.

A fish or a rose,
Fragrance or aroma,
Pleasure takes many forms.

Lord Death,
The great equalizer,
Waits patiently for our embrace.

Greet the dawn
With wonder and awe,
Earth spins for You.

Love like it is first love,
Live like it is first life,
Breathe like it is the very last.

The illusive substance
Of holy light
Pervades our very souls.

Life is good
When you are filled
With love, light, and gratitude.

Beaten up, but not down,
By rigors of life,
Parting the mists, into the dawn.

Pegasus, in an early flight,
Transported love blossoms
To the Belovéd.

The ultimate dance
Continues,
Feel the rhythm surround you.

Ascend, drop misery,
Take nothing,
Levitate on your song.

The ancient Greeks
Had profound wisdom,
Heroic stories of men and gods.

Myths reveal
Forgotten knowledge,
Seldom valued.

Do not be alarmed
If you cannot hear your song,
It will come at the right moment.

Love stirs even the old and tired;
Ever the youthful flirt,
She tickles our wayward fancy.

Just like light
Contains all colors,
We have everything we need.

Poetry is only words in a row,
Little love arrows
Reaching out to touch hearts.

Shocks, even perceived as harsh,
Can produce higher states,
Opportunity for clarity.

Moths in the light,
Fly by fast and fluttering,
Dancers whirling with delight.

The blue is so deep,
Our ceiling of air,
Rising forever to graze Heaven.

The body you currently inhabit
May contain talents or flaws,
You are here to transform all.

Truth may set our teeth on edge,
Vanity stands between us
And our need to embrace reality.

The illusion of self
Seems a cruel trick,
Only love can mend the breach.

Even this prison
Is an illusion,
The doors are open.

Turn around,
Let the light
Guide You home.

Don't think
Of what to take with you,
Don't think.

Fill days with sublime Presence,
Each moment is eternal,
Your gift to the Gods and your Self.

Though only a spark,
In my heart of heart
Soon could be a roaring fire.

Untangle the knots
That confuse you,
Soak them in conscious light.

Maybe our lives
Are inside out,
External less real than internal.

Inner actions
Can determine
External results.

The "Good Householder"
Concept,
Must also apply to inner house.

No matter your skill or artistry,
Understandings transfer
From one practice to another.

Human machinery
May be fascinating,
How much more so that of angels.

Birds commit
To a relationship,
By building a nest for babes.

Small birdlings
Are pushed from the branch,
To fly or fall.

Wings, of course,
Are an advantage,
But nothing is guaranteed.

All must take the risk,
Look up into the light,
Leap, trust Love to lift you.

Higher forces are generous
To those who are grateful,
Uncreated light exists.

Meetings:
Love shared,
In silence.

A fanfare of festival banners
Announces
A new conscious birth.

All eyes turn to
The blesséd
Breakthrough.

One gains,
We all gain,
And lose the unnecessary.

My song, your song,
Harmony of voices,
Create the soul operetta.

Each person gives and takes
What they are able,
Accepting each other is essential.

Friction cannot be avoided,
Rather it is traction,
To further love efforts.

Adorn your Self
With love garments,
Woven with extreme care.

Rest your heavy head
On the cool grass,
Growing around my temple.

Time bodies come and go,
In the timeless garden
Of eternity.

Wait on me
Ambitious One,
You cannot outrun Love.

The predawn streaks,
Herald great Father's
Dramatic approach.

Sit awhile,
Let the vines curl about your toes,
Drink the lily's nectar.

Love and light
Come in their
Own time.

Every kiss, love wink,
Sweet gesture,
Vibrates in the sensitive field.

Negative emotions can damage,
Positive ones
Spread love light in every direction.

Many steps on the path
Leading home,
And then, one giant leap.

Home: Where we began,
Where we will return,
True Self realized.

Not everything is obvious,
It would be distorted, anyway.
Truth must be sought with heart.

Even blesséd love
Can be twisted to lust,
Seek light above all.

Angels' wings surround us
At all times,
Protecting us from ourselves.

Mere knowledge
Can be depressing,
Bring heart to your prayers.

Immortality is where we belong,
Only this moment
Can show the way.

Sing 'til you drop all baggage;
Sprout wings, and
Fly home.

Inner silence,
External song,
Joy multiplied.

Hansel and Gretel
Join hands,
Dancing to your song.

Nothing is better
Than something,
Let it go.

The immortal ones
Have been there,
Done that.

Fledgling angels stumble,
Help is provided:
Elder angels understand and support.

He who loves
Is so much more fortunate,
Than he who has accumulated.

We are so careful
Of our physical body,
But neglectful of our wavering soul.

A pure harmonious soul
Can lead upwards
To rarified realms.

Positive emotions,
Unfiltered perceptions,
Help purify soul light.

Pray for gratitude,
Selfless love,
And forgiveness for all.

Palms swaying
In ocean's breeze,
Sand flying from abandoned castles.

Looking at my feet
Half in, half out,
Of white sparkling sand.

Anywhere can be
The right place,
To experience the moment.

A sudden cloud burst:
Cold drops run down my face.
Nature's variety excites new vigor.

Any activity can be used
To stimulate new efforts
To be One's real Self.

The empty is light-filled,
The full is complicated,
Light is weightless.

The tree-lined drive,
Gardens, fountains, statuary;
Beauty accompanies the journey.

New sights can freshen
The wish to be present.
Think less to see more.

Close your eyes.
The inner blank screen
Is a sensitive film: respect it.

Too much negativity
Can tint the porous soul:
Gray is the color of lead.

Take off your sandals,
Walk in the footsteps
Of men who became Gods.

We are becoming
Closer to each other,
Fewer obstacles interfering.

Reducing psychological issues
Within oneself
Makes intimacy possible.

The closer we are
To our real Selves,
The closer we will be to each other.

The golden apex
Of the pyramid
Is Love.

Like an unassembled bouquet,
Beautiful friends are strewn
Across the green sward.

My spirit lifts
To rejoice
In this gathering.

Friends have a lot to say
To each other,
And a lot more that is left unsaid.

The mystery of life and death
Is privileged knowledge,
Gods administer forgetfulness elixir.

Siren's song leads men
To destruction,
Your song leads You to love.

Raise your glass,
Drink the heady blend
To the good health of lovers.

Dark days ahead and behind,
Carry your light with you,
Always and everywhere.

Homer says poets
Are servants of the Muses;
From their mouths erupt sweet songs.

The Gods on Olympus
Look down on mere mortals
With disdain, and some compassion.

Realizing our true position
May enable
Right thinking and right action.

Help can be subtle or overt,
Best if we are sensitive to small hints,
Rather than catastrophes.

Glass shatters into tiny shards,
Great changes provide passage,
Sailing into the sea of no return.

State of being,
Transformed in an instant,
Sometimes takes years to realize.

It can feel scary
To cover new ground,
With nothing to stand on.

Fear harnessed
Can help us to proceed with caution,
Up to the leap.

Crossed swords,
August heat,
Breathing space in short supply.

Genius means
The Djinn has heard
Your call.

Muses work in harmony,
Inspiring those
Who clear their inner pathways.

We are graced with a rainbow
Of colors for our eyes;
Divine blessing for inner vision.

To will immediate presence,
Means sharing
A higher Will.

The Immortals
May laugh at our antics,
As is their privilege.

Superior beings
See further, know better,
Than mere mortals.

Compassion
Is earned through experience
And understanding.

To be more like
Immortals,
Use the tool of compassion.

Yesterday's fears
Do not exist in this moment,
Neither does our past self.

We are electric, magnetic beings,
Opposites attract,
Searching for physical wholeness.

Unification is achieved
At a much higher level,
Only with great purity of soul.

The bard and his lyre
Sing of love and pain,
A channel opens to Euterpe.

Heroes of the past
Can represent great efforts,
Needed for ascent to higher realms.

Efforts needed are mostly
To discard what is not us,
Leave imagination in the dust.

Specific instructions
Have to be minimal,
Each of us has different obsessions.

Sleep is universal,
A false sense of self;
Fear and vain self-love.

Sages from the past
Can assist immensely,
Direct help is given by Gods.

A true Teacher
Can be a channel
For higher forces to speak.

Songs of Immortality
Soar through the heavens,
Grateful for loving compassion.

Cry out
Winged words:
Heaven will hear.

Response is not always
What may be expected,
Love uses superior wisdom.

Immortals have earned
Their place in heaven,
Payment is universal.

White lilies surround
A deep blue pool of clear water,
Spotted fawns drink deeply.

So much of Paradise
Is reflected in hidden pockets
Of our very own Earth.

The adventure is enticing,
But good to remember
It is literally: life or death.

In peeling layers of an onion,
The center
Is actually nothing.

The empty cup
Allows for limitless
Possibilities.

Clear sky eyes
Survey the spacious
World of Up.

Staying awake
A consistent connection,
Not easily maintained.

If you are not your memories,
Or your thoughts, or feelings,
Who are you?

In the present moment,
You can know
Your Self.

Being supports
Every aspect of will,
Love carries force effortlessly.

Receiving cues from above
Can require the Art of Interpretation,
Or be alarmingly obvious.

Do not spend your precious time
Interpreting,
Go directly to your home: Presence.

The Play of Earth and humanity
May be nearing an end,
Transform dread and fear.

What is destined
Is not for us to judge,
Use strong emotions as fuel.

Death comes for all eventually,
The body does not comprehend
Its inevitable end.

Store up your cherished
In invisible reality,
Sustain in uncreated light.

Heart rhythm
Is the bass for spirit song.
Sing, Sing, Sing!

Lyres attend voices,
Vibrating strings, trilling echoes,
Filling sacred spaces with Love.

Songs are hymns
To those superior beings,
Who watch and care for humans.

Abstain from sleep,
Sustain
Presence.

Wordless,
Present,
Silence.

Songs burst upwards,
Gifts
Rain downwards.

Abandon yourself,
To create
Your Self.

Enter your
Inner sanctum,
Eyes and heart open.

Shelter precious
States with presence,
Move with the moment.

Nothing is forever
Except,
The eternal present.

Happily ever after
Is for fairy tales,
It could happen to you.

There is no magic solution,
But there is
Divine intervention.

The grace of light
Given to those few,
Can help light the world.

Real help is oft
Unrecognized,
We are stubborn sleepers.

Plant your feet in the earth,
Stretch your arms to the horizon,
Look up to the blue sky and sing.

As in a dream all characters
Are aspects of self;
Care for everyone around you.

Angels do not complain
About the privilege to serve
The highest among them.

Understanding our true position
Requires humility, reverence
And knowing reality.

Religion isn't bad
Unless worship
Is done in sleep.

The wind plays
The Aeolian harp,
Nature's song is pure.

Winged cherubs dress
The goddess,
In gossamer garments of stars.

We stand on the brink of immortality,
There is nowhere to go,
Drop, leap, and fly.

The unnamed
And the uncreated
Light up the nothingness.

Lavender fields
Have nothing
On Heaven's beauty.

We are so very lucky
To be here, and now,
Immerse yourself in this moment.

The divine privilege
Of presence
Makes all things full of wonder.

The barrenness of boredom
Is erased
In one instant of presence.

It is futile to wish;
Plan, strive, act,
Be: open the doors to presence.

I would touch your heart
With my words,
And lift you to your Self.

My life is limited,
But my heart sings endlessly,
In love for us all to ascend.

Do not underestimate
Your own beautifully growing
Soul.

Moments of presence
Build like a stairway
To sublime paradise.

You are loved
More every day,
There is more of You to love.

The tide crests and ebbs;
Our light is full on,
And then it fades.

Vacillating presence,
A state of being
For those on the path.

Consistency
Of light,
Devoutly to be wished.

An ocean of love
Cannot fill an
Impassioned heart.

Paradise
Looks
Like love feels.

Knowledge, Being, Wisdom;
Three very separate concepts,
Wisdom most valuable.

Knowledge of anything,
Ability to do something,
Wise enough not to.

Love can creep up,
Or take us by force,
Like a hailstorm on a sunny day.

The honeyed tones
Of vibrating harp strings
Caress white clouds, blue sky.

Rest assured
All is being done
For those few who love light.

Higher centers join
In bliss and harmony,
On the day of our birth.

Angelic songs
Rise up to heaven
In sublime celebration.

A crown of radiant glory
Sits astride
Dome of highest being.

Six strings of the lyre
Bring love to heaven,
And open Third Eye.

Self-remembering
Has a deeper meaning
For us now.

Moving through our life,
We reach the pinnacle
In realizing our true Self.

Life after death
Cannot happen without
Present life before death.

Eternal Presence
Is beyond
Life, time, or death.

Like moths to the flame,
We covet
The Teacher's fire.

The generous heart
Of a true Teacher
Kindles the flame for all his students.

Our sacred path is lit
From high above,
Each step brings us closer to home.

Distilled into pure presence,
Irrelevant disregarded,
Existence of reality appears.

Golden notes,
The Song of Songs,
Wafts through the halls of Heaven.

Egypt taught Greece,
Wisdom handed down through ages,
We are lucky to live in this one.

Beautiful art forms
Grace our lives,
Public for all who value them.

We have wisely learned
The true value of
High art impressions.

Looking deeper into
Traces of past teachers
Helps create beauty in our present.

At last,
Love
Has carried me Home.

In the end,
We will ascend,
As we are fated.

www.ingramcontent.com/pod-product-compliance
Lightning Source LLC
Chambersburg PA
CBHW031415290426
44110CB00011B/392